THE LITTLES REINDEER'S

Christmas Wish

Christmas Wish

Once upon a snowy Christmas Eve in the North Pole, there lived a little reindeer named Rosie. Rosie was the smallest and youngest member of Santa's reindeer team. While her fellow reindeer were big and strong, Rosie had a heart full of determination and dreams.

Rosie spent her days watching the other reindeer prepare for the most important night of the year when they would help Santa deliver presents to children all around the world. She longed to join them and be part of the magical journey, but she was just too small.

One crisp winter night, as Rosie gazed at the twinkling stars, she made a special wish upon the brightest one. "I wish to help Santa deliver gifts this Christmas," she whispered.

The stars above twinkled even brighter, and Rosie felt a warm, magical glow surrounding her. She knew that her wish had been heard.

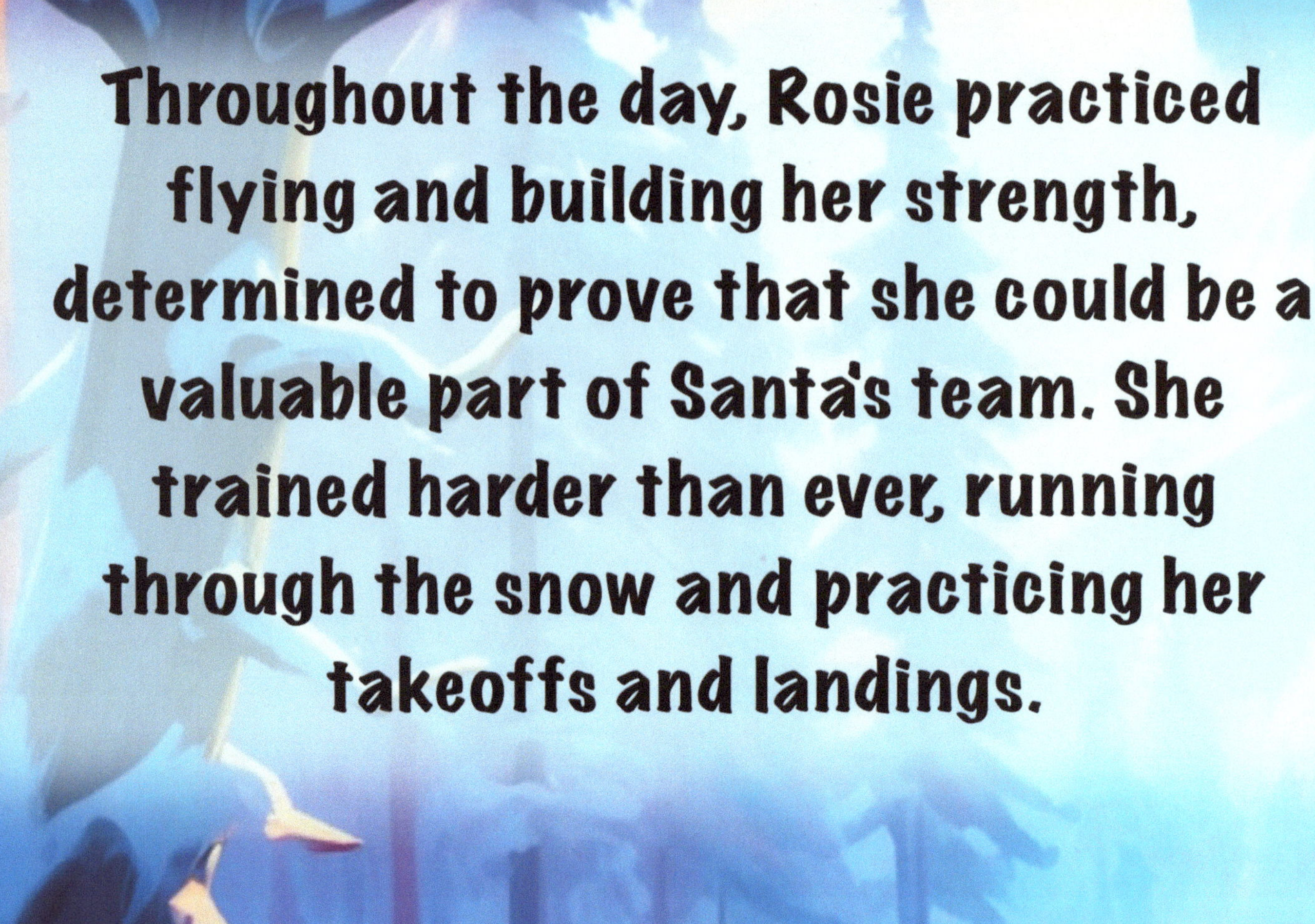

Throughout the day, Rosie practiced flying and building her strength, determined to prove that she could be a valuable part of Santa's team. She trained harder than ever, running through the snow and practicing her takeoffs and landings.

That evening, when Santa and the other reindeer were getting ready to take off, Rosie approached Santa with a hopeful heart. "Santa," she said with determination, "I've been training really hard. Please let me help you deliver presents this Christmas."

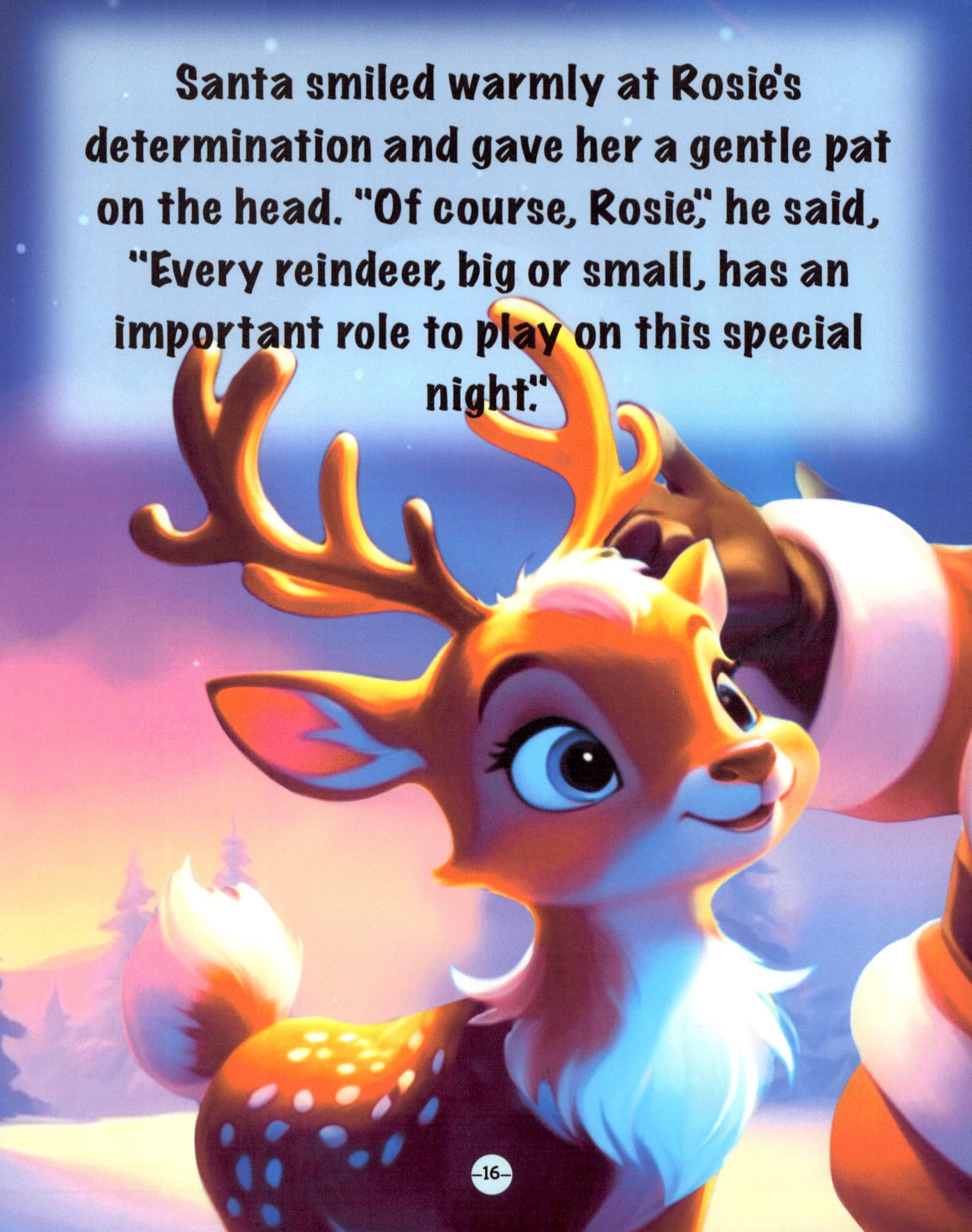

Santa smiled warmly at Rosie's determination and gave her a gentle pat on the head. "Of course, Rosie," he said, "Every reindeer, big or small, has an important role to play on this special night."

With that, Rosie was harnessed alongside the other reindeer, and they soared into the starry sky. The littlest reindeer was overjoyed to be part of the team. Together, they visited homes around the world, delivering gifts to children who had been good all year.

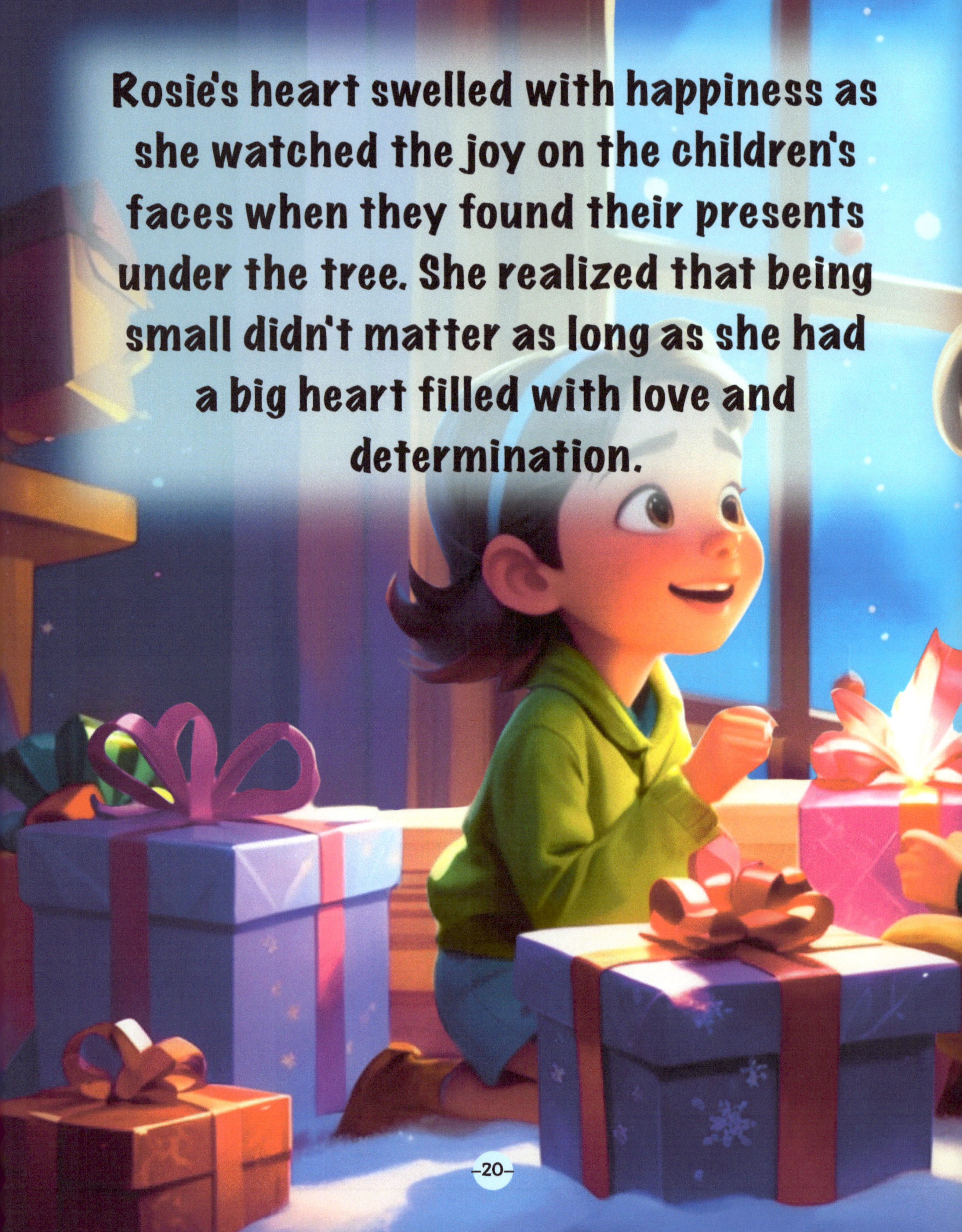

Rosie's heart swelled with happiness as she watched the joy on the children's faces when they found their presents under the tree. She realized that being small didn't matter as long as she had a big heart filled with love and determination.

As the night went on, Rosie became more and more confident in her abilities, and her fellow reindeer cheered her on. She felt like the luckiest reindeer in the world.

When the sun began to rise on Christmas morning, Rosie and her fellow reindeer returned to the North Pole, tired but filled with the warmth of the holiday spirit. Santa patted Rosie on the back and said, "You did a fantastic job, Rosie. You may be the littlest reindeer, but you have the biggest heart."

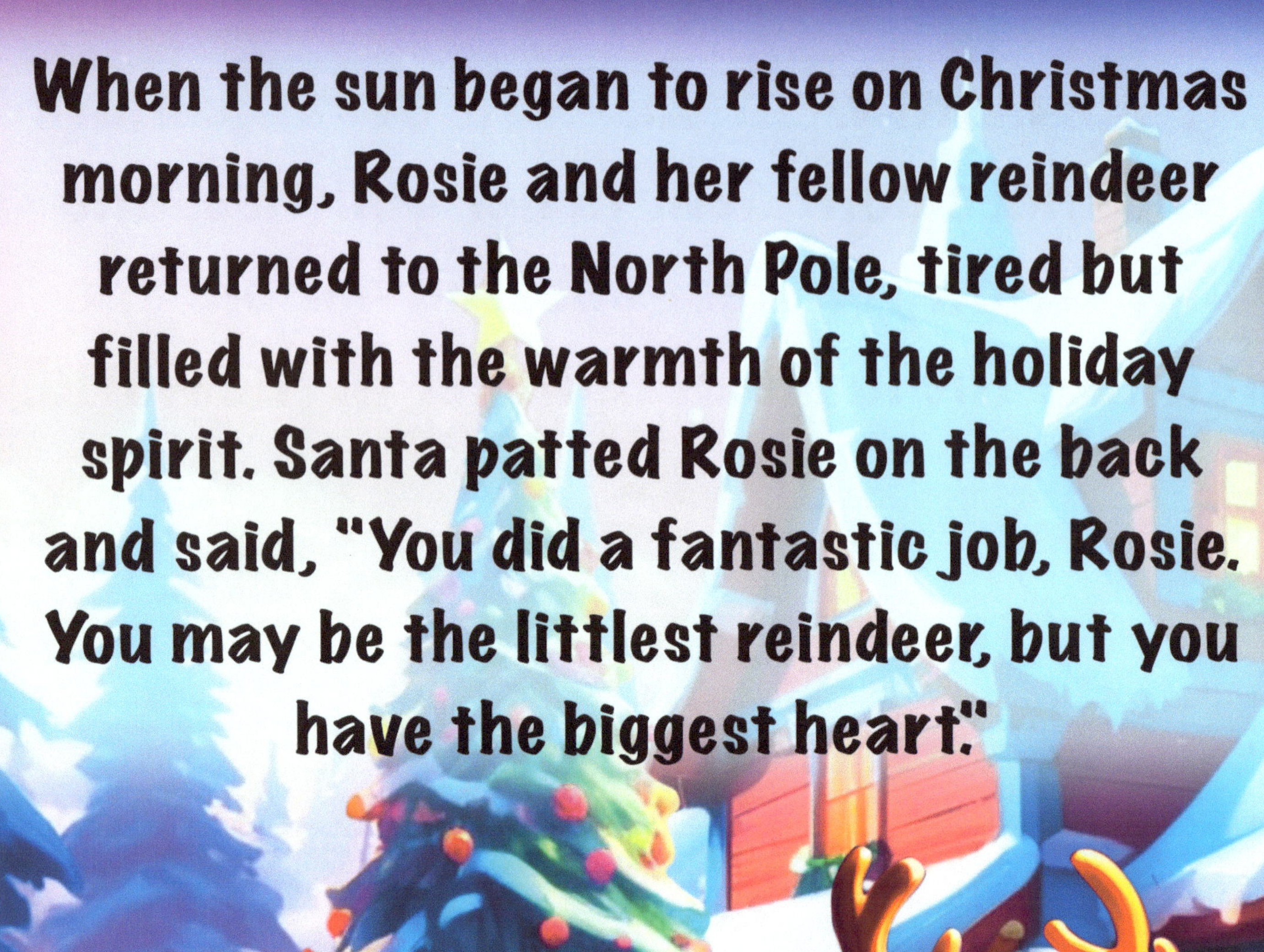

From that day forward, Rosie knew that dreams could come true, no matter how small you are, as long as you believed in yourself. And every Christmas, when she looked up at the stars, she knew that wishes could be granted with love and determination.

And so, the littlest reindeer's Christmas wish came true, and she learned that . magical gifts are the ones that come from within.